THE GIRL'S LIKE SPAGHETTI

WHY, YOU CAN'T MANAGE WITHOUT APOSTROPHES!

by
LYNNE TRUSS

illustrated by
BONNIE TIMMONS

G. P. PUTNAM'S SONS

INTRODUCTION

The apostrophe is the most helpful of all the punctuation marks. I see it as a tireless Good Punctuation Fairy, flitting above a page of words, looking for anything that's a bit of a muddle, and then waving a wand to make it clear.

I say the apostrophe is tireless because it does so many jobs, poor thing. It started out with just one simple function: to show where letters had been left out. Up above, there is an apostrophe in the word that's. It helps us see the shortened version of "that is." The title of the book has the shortened version of "the girl is."

But the apostrophe also has another job. It does its best to show when something is owned by someone or a group of people. Whenever something is owned by one person, an apostrophe appears magically before the s. So my brother's book is "the book owned by my brother"! When the thing is owned by many people, the apostrophe comes after the s, so my friends' birthdays means "the birthdays of a bunch of my friends"!

If it sounds complicated, don't blame the apostrophe. Blame the people who didn't come up with different marks for the different jobs. They were very, very shortsighted. Especially when it comes to the word its.

With the word its, two of the apostrophe's jobs crashed into each other. So someone finally decided that the word it's (with the apostrophe) would be the shortened form of "it is" and the word for "belonging to it" or "owned by it" would be its (with no apostrophe). Isn't this annoying? But it's the hardest and most annoying thing you will ever have to learn about punctuation, I promise.

I love the apostrophe, and I think we all should thank it daily for all the hard work it does on our behalf. Punctuation was invented because it was needed! And just think: Every time an apostrophe appears in the right place, the Good Punctuation Fairy is made very, very happy!

Happy punctuating,

Lynne Truss

The giant kids' playground.

The giant kid's playground.

Students' refuse to go in the garbage.

Students refuse to go in the garbage.

The dogs like my dad.

The dog's like my dad.

Ladies' lounge.

Ladies lounge.

Violets for display only.

Violet's for display only.

See the boys bat.

See the boy's bat.   See the boys' bat.

We're here to help you.

Were here to help you.

Those smelly things are my brother's.

Those smelly things are my brothers.

Jack's played here.

Jacks played here.

The tiny cat's home.

The tiny cats' home.

The shop sells boys' and girls' clothing.

The shop sells boys and girls' clothing.

Look, it's behind.

Look, its behind.

The apostrophe's like a flying comma.

The apostrophes like a flying comma.

WHY YOU CAN'T MANAGE WITHOUT THESE APOSTROPHES!

Giant kids' playground.
The apostrophe after the *s* makes *kids'* a plural noun that is possessive.

Giant kid's playground.
With an apostrophe before the *s*, *kid's* is a singular noun that is possessive.

Students' refuse to go in the garbage.
The apostrophe makes *students'* a plural noun that is possessive.

Students refuse to go in the garbage.
Without an apostrophe, *students* is a plural noun, and *refuse* becomes a verb.

The dogs like my dad.
Without an apostrophe, *dogs* is a plural noun.

The dog's like my dad.
The apostrophe makes a contraction of *dog* and *is*.

Ladies' lounge.
The apostrophe makes *Ladies'* a plural possessive.

Ladies lounge.
Without an apostrophe, *Ladies* is a plural noun, and *lounge* becomes a verb.

Violets for display only.
Without an apostrophe, *Violets* is a plural noun.

Violet's for display only.
The apostrophe makes a contraction of *Violet* and *is*.

See the boys bat.
Without an apostrophe, *boys* is a plural noun, and *bat* becomes a verb.

See the boy's bat.
The apostrophe before the *s* makes *boy's* a singular noun that is possessive (the bat belongs to one boy).

See the boys' bat.
The apostrophe after the *s* makes *boys'* a plural noun that is possessive (the bat belongs to several boys).

We're here to help you.
The apostrophe makes a contraction of *We* and *are*.

Were here to help you.
Without an apostrophe, *Were* is a verb.

Those smelly things are my brother's.
The apostrophe before the *s* makes *brother's* a singular noun that is possessive.

Those smelly things are my brothers.
Without an apostrophe, *brothers* is a plural noun.

Jack's played here.
The apostrophe makes a contraction of *Jack* and *has*.

Jacks played here.
Without an apostrophe, *Jacks* is the name of a game.

The tiny cat's home.
The apostrophe makes a contraction of *cat* and *is*.

The tiny cats' home.
The apostrophe after the *s* makes *cats'* a plural noun that is possessive.

The shop sells boys' and girls' clothing.
The apostrophes make *boys'* and *girls'* plural nouns that are possessives.

The shop sells boys and girls' clothing.
Without an apostrophe, *boys* is a plural noun.

Look, it's behind.
The apostrophe makes a contraction of *it* and *is*.

Look, its behind.
Without an apostrophe, *its* is a possessive pronoun, and *behind* becomes a noun.

The apostrophe's like a flying comma.
The apostrophe makes a contraction of *apostrophe* and *is*.

The apostrophes like a flying comma.
Without an apostrophe, *apostrophes* is a plural noun, and *like* becomes a verb.

For my mum.

—L. T.

Thank you to Ann O'Halloran and Connie Bauer of Angier Elementary School, Newton, Massachusetts, and the teachers of Santa Cruz Catholic School, Tucson, Arizona, for help with the apostrophe explanations.

G. P. PUTNAM'S SONS A division of Penguin Young Readers Group. Published by The Penguin Group. Penguin Group (USA) Inc., 375 Hudson Street, New York, NY 10014, U.S.A. Penguin Group (Canada), 90 Eglinton Avenue East, Suite 700, Toronto, Ontario, Canada M4P 2Y3 (a division of Pearson Penguin Canada Inc.). Penguin Books Ltd, 80 Strand, London WC2R 0RL, England. Penguin Ireland, 25 St. Stephen's Green, Dublin 2, Ireland (a division of Penguin Books Ltd.). Penguin Group (Australia), 250 Camberwell Road, Camberwell, Victoria 3124, Australia (a division of Pearson Australia Group Pty Ltd). Penguin Books India Pvt Ltd, 11 Community Centre, Panchsheel Park, New Delhi - 110 017, India. Penguin Group (NZ), Cnr Airborne and Rosedale Roads, Albany, Auckland 1310, New Zealand (a division of Pearson New Zealand Ltd). Penguin Books (South Africa) (Pty) Ltd, 24 Sturdee Avenue, Rosebank, Johannesburg 2196, South Africa. Penguin Books Ltd, Registered Offices: 80 Strand, London WC2R 0RL, England.

Published simultaneously in Canada. Manufactured in China by South China Printing Co. Ltd. Design by Gina DiMassi. Text set in Handwriter bold. Library of Congress Cataloging-in-Publication Data Truss, Lynne. The girl's like spaghetti: why, you can't manage without apostrophes / Lynne Truss ; illustrated by Bonnie Timmons. p. cm. 1. English language–Punctuation–Juvenile literature. 2. Apostrophe–Juvenile literature. I. Timmons, Bonnie. II. Title. PE1450.T755 2007 428.2–dc22 2006034456 ISBN 978-0-399-24706-4

1 3 5 7 9 10 8 6 4 2

First Impression